These Hands of Myrrh

These Hands of Myrrh

Poems by

Scott Ferry

Cover design by Shay Culligan
Cover painting by Leilani Ferry
Cover drawing by Scott Ferry
Author photo by Molly Ferry

ISBN: 978-1-954353-90-9

Kelsay Books
502 South 1040 East, A-119
American Fork, Utah, 84003
Kelsaybooks.com

Acknowledgments

Beautiful Cadaver Project: "Boy"

Cathexis Northwest: "Streetlights"

Gleam: The Journal of the Cadralor: "allergy"

MacQueen's Quinterly: "Bubbles the fish no longer swims," "The Japanese Andromeda," "Two days before our neighbor died," "Snow Peas"

Madness Muse Press: "Box," "Name," "Video at three months," "God as distraction"

Meat for Tea: "Corvus," "this is"

Misfit: "Don/Doff," "Last clothes," "Sons," "after confessing"

NYQ: "after finding my daughter's betta dead"

Panoply: "My dead father visits me on my birthday every year"

Praxis: "after leaving this shell"

Rye Whiskey Review: "Eviction"

Slippery Elm: "Backe, backe kuchen"

Spillway: "1994"

Thimble: "My patient does not want to live"

Verse-Virtual: "i don't remember why gilgamesh went down to the underworld," "i walk with my infant son," "Late October"

Contents

Bubbles the fish no longer swims   13
Backe, backe kuchen   15
Corvus   16
Box   17
after i find my daughter's betta dead   18
Snow peas   20
Boy   21
Name   22
i walk with my infant son   24
The Japanese Andromeda   25
Two days before our neighbor died   27
Video at three months   29
fallen toy   31
after confessing   32
i don't remember why gilgamesh went down to
     the underworld   33
1994   34
Eviction   36
Streetlights   38
My dead father visits me on my birthday every
     year   39
after leaving this shell   41
Sons   42
Last clothes   43
Don/Doff   45
My patient does not want to live   47
God as distraction   49
Late October   51
allergy   53
this is   54

"Now that I have toiled and strayed so far over the wilderness, am I to sleep, and let the earth cover my head for ever? Let my eyes see the sun until they are dazzled with looking. Although I am no better than a dead man, still let me see the light of the sun."

—Epic of Gligamesh, translated by N.K. Sandars

Bubbles the fish no longer swims

in the cup where I placed him while I changed
out the water in his tank. I yell like my arm
has just fallen off. *Lani Lani where is your fish?*

Molly come here! Where is the fish?
Where is the fish? searching the desk,
the carpet, the pencil-cup. Leilani finds
Bubbles tangled in hair in the trash can below.

I cradle him and splash him back into the cup.
His gills fan weakly, his tail waves and stills.
I have heard of betta fish jumping, but I did not believe.
I only placed a paper on top of the cup

as I left the room to sift the aqua rocks,
to run the lime-green silicone plant under scalding steam.
Lani now curls in a fetal scream on her bed.
I feel responsible so the floor keeps falling

out of my stomach, my lungs deflate and whistle.
The grief is immeasurable for a 2 inch fish,
because I forced death upon my
8-year-old daughter with my carelessness.

I tore open the safety of her womb
and now lifelessness sinks to the bottom
and inks my fingers, darkens her mouth
and her trembling lips.

But the fish stirs when we swirl the cup,
and when we drop him into his clean tank
he does struggle softly against descent.
Lani stops crying, my head tingles with hope.

I check on the fish every 10 minutes
He is going to live, he is going to live
I repeat, my daughter staring at the gills
which have somehow continued breathing.

The next morning Bubbles calmly surveys
his translucent world with a mangled tail fin.
I am no longer a murderer. And my daughter
can still walk amongst the dew.

Backe, backe kuchen

After watching a documentary
about the shark-calling people of Tembin

and the way the man sings and embraces
the muscular neck with a firm rope

then slowly releases the glassy-eyed snout,
my wife leads my daughter to bed. Lani's eyes

open underwater, searching for the edge.
Molly softly intrudes into the shallows

with milk and saffron and lard until they are both lying
on the ceiling of a bakery in Weimar, the flour

whitening the creases of their eyes. The baker
has declared! *Zucker and salz, again, yes!*

And they recline grinning in a bed of steam, or butter,
or ocean sponges, yellow as curds.

Corvus

I have been told to write about the evening migration
of thousands of crows over my house from southeast
to northwest. It seems mundane, they do it every day,

over the Petrovitsky area, over Valley Medical,
over Ikea, a black current with an unknown impetus
to a shadowy destination, maybe a soft green cemetery

with cilia growing on the banks of mossy ponds.
Maybe the dump in Orillia, maybe the beaches
of the Puget Sound, Seahurst park, or some

dark marina where bodies of salmon gape at the sky.
I notice them without noticing, my daughter
on her bike pointing up, *Daddy, the crows*

are going back home. Yes, the commute. I nod.
And the obsidian stream keeps jabbing northwest,
with calls like angry keyboards set on reverb,

but together. Sometimes they clump in cottonwood
trees along the way, holding yelling matches
among the branches. I wonder if their language

is common with all that travel this route,
or does it splinter by family, each clan
naming *enemy* and *food* and *poison*

with a separate breath.

Box

story by my daughter Leilani for a 2ⁿᵈ grade assignment

a box of gold   and diamonds
arrives at   my front door
when I open it   blue light

turns me into an   anime cat girl
a smaller box   appears
in its place made   of sapphire

and inside it   glows a lapis
necklace   with thin bands
streaked like   wind

I lift it and it   flies around
my neck   becoming a choker
I see a note   from my great

great great great   grandmother
(and I can hear   her whisper
as I read   the words)

I have passed   this down
from mother   to daughter
and now to you   so you too

will hold the power   of the wind.
And then the box   swirls into
the air   indigo and white

sparks go into   the necklace
and into my skin   and I feel
the wind   within me

rise

17

after i find my daughter's betta dead

bleached and silver on the turquoise
rocks she begins to stick pearls
into the dark openings
begins to describe how a body

without a soul is first a monster
then a wind without ribs
then just a body
and the other parts are flying

without the bones or face
just the light in the air
and she can hear
gills near her ear

the fish says good things
and mean things
he was scared
because he couldn't see

and kept spitting out his food
even after the medicine
we gave him for weeks
he knew we tried to save him

but he was scared
and then he couldn't breathe
and fell upside down
mouth gulping

until his body stopped
and a young silver fish
flipped his tail through the glass
now seeing all the bright

water

Snow peas

It's two days after Summer Solstice
raspberry light swells around the distant pines.
My snow peas which I pressed into the ground
in April now stretch and spindle up twine,
five feet high and three feet wide.
The procrastination has ended
in a combustion of cream blooms
and plump green legumes!
The taste of them takes me back
to every June and July: the crunch,
the ample juice, the sugar sweeter
than watermelon. Don't cook them,
just snap them in your teeth.
At 50 I don't get excited about much,
mostly things like this. Laughing at
my daughter's humor, rubbing my wife's back.
I try to snap a photo at the perfect angle.
But it is not the residue that matters,
nor the memory saved. It is enough
to dehisce each new pod in my mouth
right off the vine.

Boy

I have no idea how to name a baby
with a penis. All names seem false.
Maybe it is because I have never felt
completely like a man, but more of a blend

of sea and sandalwood. Certainly not
pipe tobacco and sage-burned sweat through
cologne. Plus, all the tides ruin the
leather.

Yet I have to father a boy,
teach masculinity; something like
a willingness to sacrifice without words
or a courage to protect. But, honestly,

many women do those things better.
So what is uniquely male besides
tempering the testosterone with
learned restraint and grace? Or

teaching that strength is a function
of vulnerability? In the end I just
want him not to harm. And to listen
to the wash of brine around his

deepening voice.

Name

We have planned the c-section for Friday morning,
set the middle name as my name. But her water
spills at 11:30 pm on Tuesday and she arrives
twisted and wet at the birthing center

waiting for our son to be unpackaged swiftly
after a spinal and a few jokes. We are pushed back
several hours, the doctor entering to explain another
emergency just sprang from a safe event.

My wife labors for four hours unnecessarily,
and I rub her sacrum through each attempt to push
an infant out of a perilous hatch. Once we enter
the OR and my wife vomits gurgling stew

into a tray underneath the blue tent,
the shrilling red seed comes to us, pimple-rashed
but glorious and whole. I call my sister.
She has been looking up names because we

have not decided on the first name yet.
She half-shouts *I knew it! You know today
is dad's birthday?* No, no I have forgotten.
He died in 1993. *I knew it,* she repeats.

Before I tell my wife, I already feel that my father's name
Lyle should replace my name. Even though my father
never liked his name, the pull and delivery on this exact day,
88 years after he had been extracted—this calms me.

Yes, Lyle, my wife agrees. And in Ryland's
apple-sized grimace, I see my father
looking up into the glare, the family squint
unmistakable. What other suns does he now translate?

Or these operating room spotlights screaming
through the lids? The name swallows time
like none will ever
pass.

i walk with my infant son

in the stroller through these suburban streets
which used to be an evergreen forest
and many of the douglas fir and western red cedar
still assert their stakes and hold roots
hold court despite the plasticky houses
and the asphalt where the stream used to curl
they stand 40 to 80 feet some to 100 feet
they have seen the deer and elk and bear and racoon
silently replaced by mutated wolves and tiny cougars
and mostly pale humans where smoke from pipes
and fluid talk was once sewn into the needles
and the late summer wind

and as i look down at my son
the linen sheet draped over the front of the stroller
to protect him from the sun has molded to his face
because of the gusts blowing down this manufactured
canyon and he can't see why he can't see
this whiteweave obscuring the openings to his forest
and i think we are all a bit like this
with our own fabric stuck across our voices
and we translate this group of threads and knots
as the reason for the work and the pain
and the answer rather than the bleachscript
which has covered this hill on this moist planet
in this silvered bath of stars that look cold
only because they are so far away
so far away

The Japanese Andromeda

grows taller now after we paid someone
to cut down our fruitless plum tree
which stole its sun. I enter my garage
after work and notice a champagne

bucket brimming with the opaque
white flowers from this tree
sitting on the dryer. As I open the door,
my daughter exclaims *It is time*

for the party! Don't tell Nana!
I ask *What party?* and she answers
The surprise with the confetti! Don't tell!
I am the only one leaving the house

during this plague—my wife home
with our new baby and her Mother
and Leilani. Before dinner she ushers
us out into a bath of afternoon sun,

Nana holding the baby, wife in cahoots
with Lani, me forming a circle around
the silver container. And then *Surprise!*
Ivory bells fly into the air

and shower down onto our shoulders
clinging to our hair. All day
I have evaded invisible clouds
of virus shooting from mouths

threatening to erase light and breath.
So I dig in with both hands
and loft the brittle shells up into clouds
of translucent hail which dance on the deck

25

like hummingbird bones. I feel
the moist flowers in my fingers
as the fragile skin between brightness
and silence floats around our bodies.

Two days before our neighbor died

of colon cancer, I called him into my garage
from his daily walk past our house.
Come see our new baby!
He edged in shyly because everyone
on our street had seen him drunk,
swerving on his bicycle because he got his
fourth DUI and could not drive anymore.
One afternoon he crashed his bike on the corner
next to the azalea bush and just basked
there for hours. The police were called.

He would get sober, bring smoked gouda
and salmon to our door, give me advice
on how to recover my dead lawn. Rake out
the loam, pull out the layers of diseased flesh,
reseed in April after the risk of frost
and the promise of rain. Then weeks later
he would ramble over and his liquid mouth
would chew some words like *fuck it,*
she's pissed I'm drinking again.

But today he floated slowly to the window
where my boy whimpered in the car seat
and let loose an *Awww, congratulations!*
I'll bring you some sockeye I'm about
to smoke. His skin white like the light
was already spilling out of his body,
his motions cartoonish like a ghost
pretending to walk.

The ambulance and the police
whirled red and blue two days later.

I don't judge him for his drinking,
or if that caused his intestines
to grow layers of loam over the
sorry and *sorry* and *sorry*.

Video at three months

That first deep laugh
bubbling out of your stomach
and chest, all 16 pounds of
your mass tensing with each chortle—
air taken in and spat out
in squint-eyed
gasps.

My son, there are so many things
to laugh about here and twice as many
to weep over. Let the stream of your tears
sink into the soil. The real living—
God's river of light
which fills
each

of your cells with breath—this is
laughter. And this, son, is your
first real talk with your small
silver God. Keep one hand
on this swirling
vein, this
vine

holding weightlessness through
years of blue-winged promises
disguised as words, holding
some slip of hope through
each disappointment.
May it become the
push

within your voice. From this
bright coil build your cities
of belief and faith. And, please,
son, for you and your children,
let the stream of your tears
sink into the
soil.

fallen toy

grape slices apparate on the white table
a water cup beckons to lips

and when the sacred chew monkey falls
it appears again with a swift wind in front of him

is this where it begins—
the unending disappointment

when the crush or the job or the wife or the health
falls off the crisp edge of the horizon

and no ghostly hand is there
to put everything back?

after confessing

to my wife that the reason i pace in the kitchen
and never do anything carefully
the reason every task scrapes the skin off my wrists
and the kindness out of my words and my touch
is because lately the anxiety holds my diaphragm taut
in broken harpstrings clinched in my own shaking fist
is because the sleep hasn't slept
is because i don't know how

and i've been drinking more than she knows
whiskey draining down my aorta
and once the numb stops
the frame of the room topples
on my throat again and my hands twist wires
into complex grunted phrases
wires which are meant
to play the slow steady music
or our love of my love for my children
but i don't know how

so i end up crying as i open the fridge for a beer
and my wife tells me that i don't need that
and she holds me even though i don't deserve it
and my daughter watches me weep
half-hidden by the refrigerator door

the next day i text my wife
that i have eaten week old leftovers and i am not dead yet
and she texts back *how do you KNOW we're not dead*
maybe this IS death
all i say is *because it hurts here*
but it hurts less when i feel her
feel her through this elastic wire
between us

i don't remember why gilgamesh went down to
the underworld

but i was there seven plus seven years
in the mucosa-barked madrona roots
pretending some god helped or at least
padded down the path with soft lips

pretending the sun
which was supposed to filter
through the stone path overhead
made it down here

but years strung together
and the road under the road
was still the only way from nauseous
breakfast to a sleep of painted beaks

some time in my forties i mirrored back up
into my body pulling up from under my ankles
yanking on the tendons up the long bones
into hips and ghost shoulder to socket wrapped

again—like i was twelve
before my traveler felt it necessary to burrow
i again inhabit this frame of juice and hair
because i forgave myself for all the failures

which never required forgiveness—
just breathing here skin flushed
in its own skinness the roots
now branches fruiting beards of bees

hands now blessed with
permission

1994

after Derek Annis

I didn't fall   from electrical towers
or chew teeth   in a milk-bowl
or bury my elbow   in dog jaws

                                                              no
when I lost sight   of my hands
white auras   leaked out
of bodies

I watched   pine and birch
glow vast crowns   into the clouds
while driving   down brookhurst

the dead   drifted into
my television   and covered
my math   with weeping

my skin   dismissed itself
I shook   in the shower
until the floodlamps   sobbed

the film singed   and snapped
flip   flip   flip   and the projector
swallowed the off   switch

when my friends   and family
asked what was   wrong
why I stopped   talking

I had to lie   because no one
could see   all of the halos
around trees   students   waitresses

no one could   comprehend
the gnawing   perfection of my
silence

Eviction

my father's ghost lived
in his beloved mammoth mt. condo for years

one tenant i found didn't pay rent
blew tobacco and had a dog

he never cleaned and i attempted to evict him
phoned his mother to get money

one night the other roommates woke up at 3 am
to steps and deliberate clanking of ceramic

and when they turned on the light—
dishes stacked in exact piles

even pots and pans fitted inside each other's
aluminum skins but they were the only ones there

the smoking renter still out drinking
they called me the next day said everything

looked ready to be placed into boxes
my sister and i decided my father either

wanted him to move out or was packing his
brown-green 1970s plates for a move

from this state to the next
he died so suddenly after his retirement

he never got to ski again like he was 20
single drinking until 3

he wasn't about to let someone else
inhabit his lost skin

Streetlights

The woman I dated when I was 27
used to explain that her father communicated
with her through streetlights, hallway lights,
electrical appliances of all types.
He committed suicide three years before.
I lost my father about the same time
so we navigated these dimly lit roads
together. We would be driving
in Long Beach, where all the lights
are tinged bitter orange,
and she would snap her head
towards a light that extinguished right
before we passed, then I would feel
her soften, sadden, close her
eyes with a secret grin,
reaching through the fabric
of night to hold one darkened
hand.

My dead father visits me on my birthday every year

this year it is when i drive
down talbot rd on my way to work
he unfolds his glinting body all over my torso

and the cottonwoods along the road
glow magnetic and my eyes slip with water
and he is telling me how much he loves

his grandson and that my road will
tear like printer paper
in places but to keep driving

and keep forgiving what time does
and that my wife will stand me taller
and my daughter cries music and art

and my mother will die soon
and my sister will help her come to
him when her clock stops

all of this happens in about 30 seconds
i have heard there is no time
on the other side so how does he know

when to dive into the lashing current
to find me in a vehicle
and give me half a minute

of whispers which wet
the wheel? does he watch
the bloodied river

screech and roll until i am
drenched enough
to listen?

after leaving this shell

lift now with the hospital exhaust—
in light the cities blur

arriving i am welcomed, mouthless—
i step stingless over snow

father, father i missed you—
how do i unbreak this throat?

can i sing to my children
through these sumac roots?

my wife, can i hold you
with these hands of myrrh?

Sons

When I care for an elderly man in the hospital
and the son comes to pick up his father
I see how the father's relationship with suffering
and laughter and hope amidst pain

has transmitted to the younger.
Has he preached to the son and did
the son decide to digest the sermon
or choose other gods?

85% of the time the mythology remains unbroken:
if the father pulls on the lines keeping him alive with disgust
and frustration, the son will rail on about the traffic
and the parking.

If the father jokes about how the surgery for his bladder
didn't make his manhood grow, as was promised,
the son will confess that the surgery did not make
his father mute, as was promised.

But there are those sons who either have chewed
on their own dark tobacco until it has blistered their fingers
or have drank from the shine of decent friends
until they are buoyant.

So I remember, most times, how to interact with my God
in front of my daughter, and now my son.
I don't ever want to see them curse
all the gifts in their hands.

Last clothes

Today I compressed a man's chest standing on a stool.
They have already been trying to save this patient
for 45 minutes when I am summoned to help because
the compressors are getting tired.

People look destroyed in the room,
pale skin, glances downward, a confusion
of blood, IV bags and lines, and machines
with one sunken rack of bruises on the table

in front of me. I begin pumping, keeping up
100 beats a minute. His chest has no more
intact ribs, I am certain, but the code
continues and I have two minutes

until the next pulse check. My scrub pants
never want to stay up, and today is no exception.
So, now my pants slink halfway down my cheeks
and my crack enters the room like a joke

at a funeral. I want so badly to yank up my pants
but I cannot. I want to call out to someone, anyone
to lift them up for me, but I cannot. Then I think,
is it more disrespectful to bare my ass

in the service of this man, or to ask for assistance
in this time of stoic duty? I choose to continue
unabated. The next round I pull them so high
my socks show in their entirely.

The man regains a pulse for about 2 minutes,
there are scattered claps and muted cheers.
Then the blood pressure drops again and so
does the pulse and the code is stopped.

This patient had no reason to die, just quit
breathing under moderate sedation. The doctors walk
ahead of me to tell the daughter. I gather the last clothes
he wore in a plastic sack, wait for the doctors to

say the words.

Don/Doff

We are mandated to go to PPE training
where we prepare for all the infected patients
who will blister from the walls of this hospital—
fluid-filled and pale.

The instructor exudes calm professionalism
as we watch a video on how to scour our hands:
wring fists together like two sumo wrestlers,
twist around the trunk of each thumb,
steeple up the empty roofs and quake,
pinch the digits together, and rub
on the palms as if starting a fire.

Then we go to an imaginary droplet
room in which a person (our neighbor
our friend our grandmother) is drowning.
I volunteer and attempt to joke
Oh great, I got the hardest scenario!
and everyone returns a magnetic hostility.
The teacher retorts *This is actually the easiest one.*

Don: gown, tie behind back, mask N95. Wait—
wash hands: squeeze/tree/church/clutch/burn.
Gloves up over cuffs. Face shield with plastic
barrier over eyes. Enter room facing the ill.
Do patient care (as if that was the easiest part).
Back away from the contaminated area.
Wash gloved hands: wrest/whorl/spire/pinch/flame.
Wipe the doorknob and threshold. Keep your dirty
face toward the body (remember: dirty to dirty).
Exit the door.

Doff: gown, like pulling off charred skin.
Roll it up into a wet heart.
Pull soiled gloves over and discard.
Wash hands: crush/circle/tent/curl/excoriate.
Doff outer mask. Keep facing the door.
(Dirty to dirty.) Make sure your eyes are dry
before removing your inner mask.

My patient does not want to live

My job today is to sit with him for 12 hours
so he doesn't try to open the blood or close the air.
He has not wanted to eat, but this morning
he allows French toast and sugar free syrup
to nourish him. He even drinks his milk.

When the young doctors arrive he barely answers them.
The mid-20s man asks *How does your body feel today?*
And my patient answers: *It lets me know it is still here.*
He throws a few more answers onto the ground
and the doctors shrug at me and slink out perplexed.

My patient is in his 60s, has bilateral
AKAs (above knee amputations),
doesn't feel like defecating more than
once a week. I ask him what he wants
to watch, he chooses a paranormal investigation

show. *Are you still here? How many of
you are still here?* the young researcher
asks into the dark, night vision film
rolling blank blue and yellow.
A thunderous moan comes out of the corner

and they all spin around, monitors flickering.
I ask my patient, *Have you had any experiences
with ghosts?* He nods, *Oh, yes.*
I inquire, *Did you grow up in a haunted
house or something?*

Nope. And then he just looks at me
and when I look back he pretends
he is staring at something behind me,
the whiteboard with his food intake, his urine
output displayed in dry-erase. I want to hear

his stories, I want to release his ghosts
which spin opaque behind the glass,
which inhabit his body
still.

God as distraction

1. *God damn it!* my father bellows to my mother
and sister through the drywall and cement i'm sure
all the way to the off-white house to our south—
silence we steal and strawberries along the borders
and to the white-haired lady in the cream house
to the north with the cacti in rock and the kitchen smell
of burnt frosting with her 5 cats—i hope to God
she doesn't hear him

2. My daughter refuses to turn on her zoom screen
because her classmate (who she struck with a tree branch
yesterday when he wouldn't leave her sacred rock)
is now talking about not hitting people on the playground
she weeps in a curl of muscle and all i can do is raise my voice
lift her shaking into her room where she screams
when i shut the door and listen to the recording
of my father in the electric hallway

3. My last year of teaching the anger became a cramp
that cancered my throat when the girl in my class began crying
in the conference room her teeth slicing my accusations
of her not complying with my rules—my skin flat deflating
in ribbons as she cried and her parents silent
and the Assistant Principal handed her a tissue and i think
now what kind of monster makes a girl weep in front
of her parents? what empty wind clears an airless room?

4. The Minarets tooth through the white shoulders and hips
below Mammoth Mountain i see my father's sunglassed eyes
in the March sun i notice a rare grin he clicks his orange
boots into skis my gloved hands loose before gripping poles
and pushing off again i can almost forget there were breaths

between the clinching and if he knew a God it was here
in these short delays outside the gondola—the stolen
panoramas of granite and tooth—the distracted
connection of earth and sky

5. After he dies he keeps coming to me in the bathroom
(either while i am on the toilet or standing in the shower)
just long enough for the tasks in my hallways to stop
screaming just long enough to be distracted
by the camera's soft light blurring my insides and to feel
his calm rinse into the room (a calm i wish he had allowed
himself for more than three breaths) and i think
on my daughter and her temper and how to soothe
her nerves with an electric glove—how to teach her
to love her own hands

Late October

1. ice points the lawn with mirrors
blinking as i step past in my sandals
i grip the recycling taste the smell of frost
the poppy stems which spread as weeds
still erect resplendent—the hose chokes
with slush as i rinse the remaining carrots
which i pull from the earth's glittering gums

2. my mother reclines on the family room couch
the velour one we never use in the room
which stays vacant until recently when the yelling
cranked off like a creaking faucet and a distance
has spread words apart—a forest where spruce
and fir have been thinned
with no plans of replanting

3. with a child and now a baby i have no time to yank
the dandelion and red clover from between strawberries
onions or peas so i roll black fabric over the growth
gauging holes where the wanted vegetables will be allowed
to grow—i hold the dark sheets down with rocks
some rusted pins—at intervals peppermint and chamomile
emerge from the edges and the torn places

4. my son flips one twisted stretch of muscle
on the changing table even with the purple-red lion
wet in his gums he whirls like an otter in kelp
i grip his legs pull the swollen diaper off with a swift
motion ripping one side off—he stops—startled
i don't think i hurt him but i am ashamed
that i have exerted too much against his fragile will

5. first frost and the roses will be cut
shears snap through wiry stems and sparse burgundy leaves
some slice cleanly as thin acquaintances some resist the blade
i cannot keep any flowers even the newly opened
because they will die out here and this is the season for death—
but i hold two bruise-red buds curled in utero carry them
into the room where we eat—where we continue to live

allergy

1. as if she skims on a swan her lithe arms
wave towards the passing cars—camping headlight
nausea yellow on her head—shopping cart empty
lavender blouse tracing each sweep

2. a woman tends a shrine of too-red roses
and metallic heart balloons on the side of talbot road
the traffic does not break her deliberate breathlessness
as her tender hands place hollow membranes into earth

3. cinder and histamine bulge in her lip
my daughter swallows the blood-colored benadryl
to keep the flood from churning down her trachea
her eyes well with clear dark milk

4. the spines of the rocking chair separate
like teeth on threads oak sternum nearly slips off ribs
but we trust and settle into this daily breaking—
lulling with down-eyed songs to this kicking bird

5. this night i hear a persimmon flush of laughter
outside lifting magenta and thyme into the dark—wait—
are they weeping? a pause like a grey egg cracks
in a shriek—another cry another laugh skips
like silk down the jeweled street

this is

the poem inside the poem inside the poem
i write when everyone is asleep
when dishes have stopped dripping on the rack
when the dryer in the garage clanks its last zipper

when the body of a hundred tasks creaks into the chair
when the thought of sex snores softly in the dark
when all i dislike about others releases into a long exhale
when all i abhor about myself slides under the door

i tire of holding up these grievances
like a dust-drunk Moses
so i drop them like chalk into sand
and they whisper away like scarabs

God could talk but i am not listening
i even let the switchboard of programmed responses
alarm its empty lights in the hallway
the cat doesn't care

sometimes i just wish i could stay here—
a blue whorl of breath
inside breathless
dark

About the Author

Scott Ferry helps our Veterans heal as a RN in the Seattle area. He has two books: *The only thing that makes sense is to grow* (Moon Tide, 2020) and *Mr. Rogers kills fruit flies* (Main St. Rag, 2020). He also has a chapbook upcoming in 2022 from Ethel titled *The Sea of Marrow.* You can find more at ferrypoetry.com.

www.ingramcontent.com/pod-product-compliance
Lightning Source LLC
Chambersburg PA
CBHW031153090426
42738CB00008B/1317